Kingfell Guide KF912

Second Edition: 2013

Crisis Management Planning

Threat Identification & Mitigation, Preparation, Response & Recovery

Crisis Management Planning

Copyright © 2013 Kingfell

All rights reserved.

ISBN: 1484920058
ISBN-13: 978-1484920053

CONTENTS

Preamble 1

Introduction 3

Scope 3

Terms and definitions 4

1   General Considerations 5

2   Crisis management and risk management 9

3   The crisis management process 11

4   Threat identification and mitigation 13

5   Threat Analysis 19

6   Threat Mitigation 24

7   Pre-crisis Preparation 27

8   Responding to a Crisis 32

9   Recovering from a Crisis 38

10   Testing and Exercising the Plan 40

11   Review and maintenance of the plan 42

About the Author 43

TABLE OF FIGURES

Figure 1: Crisis and Risk Management - working together 10

Figure 2: Crisis management plan flow chart 12

Figure 3: Identification of possible outcomes 19

Figure 4: Risk based objectives matrix 21

Figure 5: Probability / Impact Matrix 25

Figure 6: Crisis response profiles 33

Note: All figures are the copyright© of Kingfell.

ACKNOWLEDGMENTS

I would like to thank my colleagues at Kingfell, past and present, for some of the ideas that I have taken on board. I would also like to thank all those I have met in the fire and resilience profession, mostly in the UK and USA, who have inspired me to write this Guide.

Paul Bryant

PREAMBLE

Kingfell has been involved with fire safety and fire engineering since its formation in 1995.

In 2007, it explored the relationship between fire safety and crisis management. As part of its research, it was found that there were numerous books and guidance documents on crisis management but there was probably still a need to provide a document that sets out the basic elements of crisis management in a clear and concise format such as that normally found with codes of good practice.

Paul Bryant, founder and CEO of Kingfell, decided to explore the subject with the help of two colleagues experienced in crisis management who then worked with him at Kingfell. One of the concerns he found was that crisis management meant different things to different people. He visited exhibitions involved with crisis management and resilience and found that they largely concentrated on IT back-up and support systems and little on overall crisis management concepts. Another sector of crisis management was more to do with public relations and the control of messages to the outside world in the event of an incident or event – good or bad.

This Guide was written by Paul and incorporates the results of his findings. It uses recognised crisis and incident management procedures together with ideas and concepts he developed over the last few years. A first Code version of this document was prepared by Kingfell in 2010 as a downloadable PDF format document.

This edition has been completely reformatted for publication both as a printed book and as an ebook. It has also been changed from a Code to a Guide to reflect its advisory status. Parts of the text have been amended and additional information on objectives setting has been included.

The Guide is intended to assist with the preparation of a crisis management plan for organisations of all types and of all sizes. A Chapter is included covering the analysis of threats to the organisation with the objective that the final plan becomes more meaningful and relevant. It is prepared in a format to allow use internationally.

This Guide has been drafted and developed by Paul Bryant for Kingfell, which retains its ownership and copyright. It does not purport to include all necessary provisions of a contract. Users are responsible for its correct application. Furthermore, Kingfell accepts no responsibility or liability for the outcome of incidents where this document was partially or wholly used.

This edition is KF912 – Second edition: 2013. This Guide uses UK English spelling.

INTRODUCTION

The term "crisis" can have different meanings to different persons or organisations. A crisis for one company could start when their share price plummets due to activities outside of their control. Confidence in the company's abilities may reduce as a consequence, which may, in turn, lead to demise in their ability to trade. This could be seen an opportunity to other companies to turn the situation to their advantage. Similarly, a crisis may appear not to be an immediate problem but could swiftly lead to one. For example, a leaking tap in a museum basement may not be deemed to be a crisis but when major works of art happen to be stored nearby, and could be subjected to water damage, then this could be judged to be a potential crisis.

A crisis can derive from a single incident or event, from a number of events working together or against each other, or from a change in externally created conditions. It may be slow building or instantaneous or may not even be apparent for some time. Consequently, planning for every conceivable form of crisis is likely to be extremely difficult to do so there is merit in assessing the type of threat that an organisation is more likely to face.

By preparing a crisis management plan, an organisation will gain a detailed understanding of the threats and corresponding risks that face its business, its vulnerabilities to certain types of risk, and the level of resilience it can introduce by adopting a framework, such as that proposed in this Guide.

SCOPE

This publication provides guidance for the formulation of a crisis management plan. It covers guidance to assess and analyse the type of threats that may be faced and how to mitigate these threats by a combination of prevention and protection techniques. The resultant exposure to a crisis should then be covered by the crisis management plan encompassing preparation, response, recovery and testing.

This document is written to apply to most types of organisation and should be used as deemed appropriate to the circumstances of the organisation.

TERMS AND DEFINITIONS

For the purposes of this Guide, the following terms and definitions apply.

Crisis - An event, incident or set of circumstances that has been determined to be an unexpected and/or unwanted occurrence, with potentially severe consequences.

Friends and Family- A term used to describe those who may have an emotional attachment to those affected by a crisis.

Organisation - A term referring to a company, group of companies, authority or any other body that could be affected by a crisis.

Resilience- The ability to continue to operate through adverse conditions, or to recover quickly and return to normal operating conditions.

Resources - Personnel, information, equipment, plant, vehicles, etc. required to assist with the management and control of a crisis.

Risk management – Means taken to control risks to a manageable level.

1 GENERAL CONSIDERATIONS

Our understanding of what constitutes a crisis can vary considerably based on a personal, organisational, national or international perspective. The term "crisis" is normally associated with a disaster of some kind but it could also be associated with conditions creating an opportunity or reassessment of conditions.

It is recognised that there are a number of key factors associated with crisis management and control, which are:

• A crisis can derive from a single incident or event, from a chain of events, from a change in circumstances or from a short-term or slowly building situation that leads to a specific "tipping point".

• The understanding of what is a crisis is, at what point a scenario becomes a crisis, will continuously vary between persons, organisations, periods of time and many other transient and longer term factors.

• The proper handling of a crisis can limit its impact both in terms of severity and duration.

• Mishandling of a crisis can lead to secondary crises that could potentially be worse than the initial crisis and could take resource away from the initial crisis.

• A properly managed crisis scenario relies on effective internal and external communications.

For the purpose of this Specification, a crisis is divided into three basic types:

1. Incident based crises; where a specific tangible condition arises quickly, normally within a contained geographical area. Examples include a major fire; loss of communications; process accident; explosion and terrorist attack. Note that some major incidents are not normally immediately referred to as a crisis (e.g. train crash) but could become a crisis either due to additional factors (e.g. chemical spillage due to the impact, or that VIPs were aboard the train) or to the mishandling of the incident leading to an uncontrolled situation.

2. Event based crises; where a single or multiple change in conditions may lead to an adverse direct or indirect impact. Examples include earthquake; pandemic "flu" outbreak; heat wave; change of government; currency devaluation and staff lottery win.

3. Crises arising from a change in circumstances; this is where a more gradual change in conditions may have an adverse direct or indirect impact. Examples include economic recession; increased terrorist activity and global warming.

A crisis management plan is designed to ensure that, if and when a crisis scenario occurs, an organisation has the relevant systems in place to respond quickly and efficiently with the objective to limit the impact and duration of the crisis, and to prevent secondary crises occurring from inappropriate actions undertaken whilst handling the original crisis. The plan is to provide additional degrees of resilience to an organisation.

It is vital that those entrusted to prepare a crisis management plan have the necessary levels of competence to undertake the task professionally and thoroughly. The level of competency required will be commensurate with the expected complexity of the assignment, but the person, or team should have the following credentials:

• A good understanding of crisis issues and their management with regard to the organisation in question.

• An appropriate knowledge of legislation with respect to the various aspects associated with crisis management and control.

• Appropriate qualifications, training and / or experience in crisis management and control issues.

• Knowledge of relevant national regulations and codes with experience of their application.

One way of validating competency is to ensure that those preparing the plan, or those approving the plan are members of a relevant professional body at an appropriate level.

Prior to formulating the plan, a panel should be set up to guide the persons tasked with its preparation. All parts of the organisation including those involved with core services and of supporting activities should be represented at the panel. The panel may include:

- the person(s) preparing the plan.
- persons responsible for communications and information systems within the organisation.
- persons representing the fire, safety and security interests of the building or organisation.
- persons involved with other key activities including finance, commerce, operations and public relations.
- persons representing other building or organisation interests affected by the plan (e.g. human resources, heritage issues, facilities management, etc).
- relevant regulatory authorities.
- insurers.

The panel should meet at key stages of the plan development. These stages may include:

- planning meeting(s).
- meeting(s) to consider specific issues, such as objectives setting, threat assessments, building issues, etc.
- technical meetings to consider aspects such as resource requirements.
- review meetings at key milestones to review work stages.

All interested parties may not be required to be at all meetings although it is recommended that they do attend the initial and milestone meetings. The meetings should normally be chaired by those preparing the plan as they should have the relevant knowledge and experience to ensure all factors have been appropriately considered.

Before commencing with the analysis, all persons involved with the plan should agree the scope of the plan. Key to this process will be to agree:

- what is to be specifically included and excluded from the plan.(This could be as a result of the threat / risk analysis and mitigation assessment identified in this Guide).

• the parameters that will be used as acceptance criteria. This could vary between organisations but could be simply to meet with a basic level of compliance or to cater for specific issues raised by internal or external parties. These criterions may be subject to amendment as a result of initial investigation, particularly as a result of assessing the objectives for the organisation. In these cases, amendments should be mutually agreed by all interested parties.

• what assumptions may be made at the outset of the plan. Similarly, a process may be required to accept and approve subsequent assumptions made throughout the stages of plan preparation.

2 CRISIS MANAGEMENT AND RISK MANAGEMENT

Risk management, sometimes referred to as "Total Risk Management", is a process increasingly used by organisations to protect themselves against unwanted events. Organisations may already be aware of a number of their risks and may have steps in place to manage the risks. Risk management could include the following areas:

- Life safety and preservation.

- Asset protection and preservation, including buildings, property, equipment, machinery, etc.

- Business protection and continuity.

- Environmental protection and preservation.

Threats to the organisation can come in various forms and at any time. Crisis management involves the taking of appropriate actions in the relatively rare instance when risk management, encompassing prevention and protection, is not sufficient to cater for the identified threat. In effect, a crisis management plan provides the glue to ensure survivability when a threat cannot be handled in any other way.

This concept is illustrated in Figure 1. The figure shows the four typical forms of risk management as described above. Where threats of a certain type cannot be protected against by risk management systems alone, the crisis management plan could shield the organisation from the full impact of the threat.

Prior to the preparation of a plan, and to make the plan more appropriate to the type of crises the organisation may face, it is recommended that a threat assessment is undertaken. By following through a process as given in Chapters 4 and 5, a number of possible outcomes that may form the basis of a crisis can be assessed. These identified threats or risks to the organisation can be handled in one of three ways:

1. Prevention; by identification of the potential root causes of the threat and taking steps to remove the identified risks at their source, such that the probability of

occurrence is reduced.

2. Protection; by using processes or systems to minimize the impact of the identified risks.
3. Preparation, response and recovery; by taking management and control actions prior to, during, and after an occurrence deemed to be a crisis.

The first two items may be covered by appropriate levels of risk management. The third is an integral part of a crisis management plan.

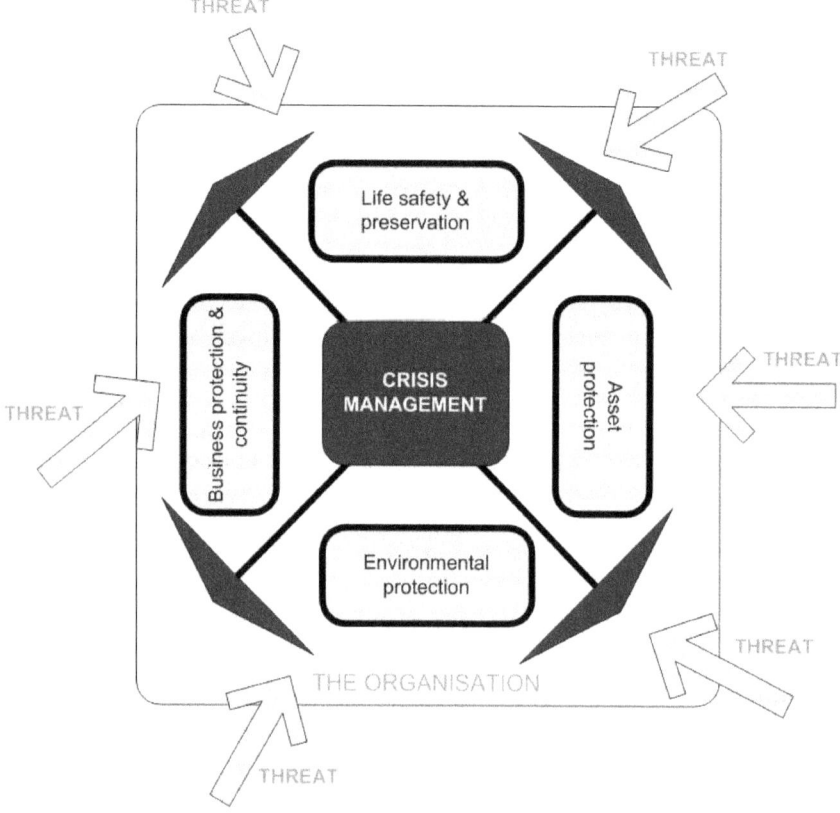

Figure 1: Crisis and Risk Management - working together

3 THE CRISIS MANAGEMENT PROCESS

The crisis management process establishes a workflow and context which allows the organisation to respond to crisis appropriately.

A crisis management plan should be an agreed set of principles and guidance designed to ensure a satisfactory level of loss prevention and resilience. A typical plan may consist of the following parts:

Corporate policy statement: This is a statement from those at a higher level in the organisation (such as Company Directors) of their commitment to the formulation and implementation of a crisis management plan. This could incorporate the key objectives for the plan and any performance criteria or expectation.

Preparation for a crisis: This will cover a series of measures that have been agreed and can be put quickly into place in the event of a crisis. Such measures will include a command and control structure; communication systems; procedures and instructions to be followed; supporting information and intelligence to be used, resource requirements, etc. This is covered in Chapter 7.

Response to a crisis: This will provide a process to be followed in the event of a crisis and should include the steps to be taken, the decision making process, use of resources, etc. This is covered in Chapter 8.

Recovery from a crisis: This will provide a process and a list of considerations to be followed to minimize the longer term damage or disruption created by the Crisis. This is covered in Chapter 9.

Testing and maintaining the plan: This will provide details of how often the plan should be tested, reviewed and maintained. It should include for a positive feedback and improvement cycle. This is covered in Chapter 10.

It is recommended that a full and thorough threat analysis is undertaken to identify those threats that can be contained by risk management and those that may require a specific response as covered by a crisis management plan. This Specification identifies six groups of threat as illustrated in Figure 2. From the threat analysis, the key residual risks identified will need to be catered for by the crisis management plan.

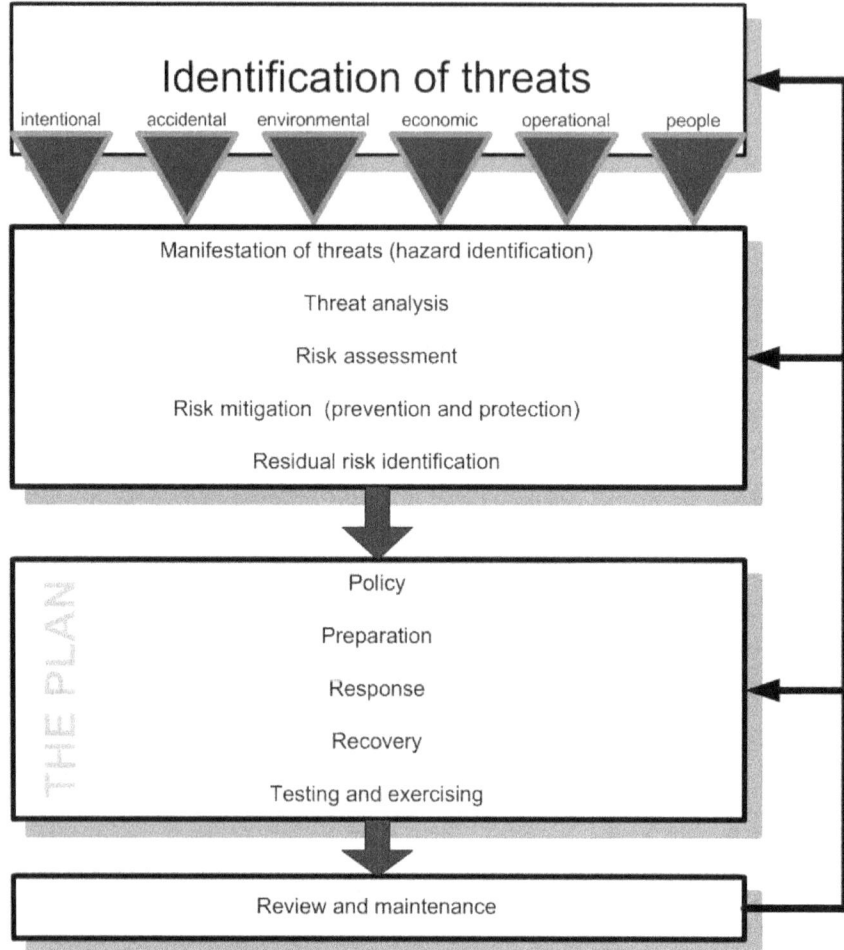

Figure 2: Crisis management plan flow chart

4 THREAT IDENTIFICATION AND MITIGATION

A crisis management plan can only be effective and complete if all determining factors have been properly considered. These are the factors that should be thoroughly investigated by a combination of research of relevant data and records, by liaising with key personnel to derive relevant information, by undertaking site surveys and by evaluating the impacts of previous relevant crises.

In some cases, the determining factors may be limited, possibly because previous assessments have been undertaken and can be used to support the plan, or the scope of assessment has been limited to consideration of specific aspects only. It is recommended that the extent of assessment is agreed at the initial planning meetings.

A threat assessment can help in the focus of what could happen given a certain set of circumstances. In this Guide, these are referred to as "threats" and are allocated into six distinct groups as shown in Figure 2 and in the following clauses. A thorough threat assessment will help focus on the level of exposure an organisation may face to a crisis. Given below are some considerations for each of the threat types. An assessment can then be made of how each of the threats could manifest themselves to, or within, the organisation.

Intentional threats or actions

The ability to understand how and where an intentional action, or actions can lead to a crisis, is paramount to assist with the managing of a crisis. In some cases, even the *threat* of intentional action, without the action being instigated, can lead to a crisis scenario. It is in the planning for, and the reaction to, the threat where the severity and duration of the subsequent crisis can be minimized. The following considerations could help in identifying significant threats. Note that the list is not exhaustive.

• Are there any groups or individuals who have shown aggressive behaviour towards the organisation?

• Does the organisation or individuals within the organisation support any political or religious causes that could be deemed to be in conflict with outside individuals, groups or organisations?

• Has the organisation made any decisions that could disadvantage any individuals, groups or organisations?

• Could the organisation be associated with national or sector based activities that could cause offence to other individuals, groups, organisations or nations?

• Could actions against staff, subcontractors or suppliers result in threats against the organisation?

• Could the actions of, or against, a neighbouring organisation, or an organisation based in the same sector lead to increased risk of intentional action against the organisation in question?

• Does a potentially hostile organisation or group demonstrate a clear or developing capability to deliver a threat to the organisation?

From the consideration of the possible causes of an "intention" derived crisis, a review of how the action could lead to an incident should be ascertained together with the possible types of incident that could result. In the case of intentional threats or actions, the manifestation could be anything from theft and damage to property to more serious issues such as grievous bodily harm, kidnap, blackmail, murder, arson and explosion.

Accidents

Accidents may range from minor mistakes to major disasters. Some accidents and types of accident may have a greater or lesser probability of occurring and a greater or lesser impact. Consequently, a full risk assessment can help identify the potential for accidents and how they could impact on individuals, the organisation and on the wider community. The following considerations could help in identifying significant threats. Note that the list is not exhaustive.

• What are the possible accident types that could be attributed to the organisation?

• Does the organisation have a health and safety policy? If so, is it adhered to?

• What organisational data is available on accident rates and types? Is there a formalized review process that can help identify accident reoccurrences?

- Is there any industry sector data on the type and frequency of accidents and the potential of a crisis deriving from the accidents?

- Has the organisation made any changes in operations or structure that could potentially lead to accidents that may not have previously occurred?

- How could accidents from external personnel or organisations impact on the organisation?

- Are there any "chain reaction" accident types in the organisation where one accident could lead to further incidents?

From the consideration of the possible causes of an "accidental" derived crisis, a review of how the action could lead to an incident should be ascertained together with the possible types of incident that could result. In the case of accidents, the manifestation could be anything from minor injury and individual fatalities through to process failure, fire and explosion.

Environmental threats

Environmental threats can usually be divided into two types:

- Threats that are highly likely to re-occur, even if the frequency and impact cannot be readily ascertained.

- Threats that may be totally or partially unexpected.

Organisations based within "high risk" areas such as earthquake zones and flood plains are more likely to have taken steps to minimize the impact of such an event. However, there will be environmentally derived events that could directly affect or impact on any organisation, some of which may not be readily envisaged. For this reason, a thorough consideration of possible threats should be undertaken in all cases. The following considerations could help in identifying significant threats. Note that the list is not exhaustive.

- What are the known environmental threats that could impact on the organisation? How have these been accounted for?

- What are the potential environmental threats that could impact on the organisation yet have not been accounted for?

- How could longer term changes in climate affect the type,

frequency and impact of the known or potential environmental threats? Could new threats be introduced in the coming years as a result of climate change?

• Are there any activities undertaken by the organisation that could increase the risk of an environmental threat?

• Could the activities or actions of other organisations, communities or nations increase the risk of an environmental threat?

From the consideration of the possible causes of an "environmentally" derived crisis, a review of how this could lead to an incident should be ascertained together with the possible risks that could result. In the case of the environment, the manifestation could be anything from increased rainfall impacting on operations to landslide, wildfires, earthquakes and tsunamis.

Economic Threats

Every organisation will be vulnerable to a greater or lesser degree by changes in economic conditions. There may be a direct impact to business trading or there may be more subtle changes where the global economy or supply/demand relationships change over time. The following considerations could help in identifying significant threats. Note that the list is not exhaustive.

• How well financially controlled is the organisation in terms of accounting data, cash flow, etc? What are the areas in which the business is exposed?

• What are the key external economic threats to the organisation and the industry?

• What stage of the economic cycle is the organisation and industry operating within? How could this introduce additional pressures to operations?

• What are the factors that could adversely impact on the economic conditions of key clients and suppliers?

• Could changes in economic conditions exert additional competitive forces for the organisation?

• Are there any external organisations, bodies, unions etc. who could impact on the economic conditions of the company?

From the consideration of the possible causes of an economic derived crisis, a review of how this could lead to an incident should be ascertained together with the possible types of incident that could result. The manifestation could be anything from reduction in profit, loss of market share to bankruptcy.

Threats to and from operations

Operations, i.e. the day to day core activities of the organisation, can be affected by crisis caused by both internal and external situations. Operations could also introduce threats to the organisation. The following considerations could help in identifying significant threats. Note that the list is not exhaustive.

• What are the key elements of failure in operations? Have they been risk assessed? How have these risks been mitigated to date?

• How will a partial or complete power failure impact on the organisation?

• How resilient are the existing IT and communication systems? What would be the impact of partial or total failure?

• What aspects of the supplied good or services of the organisation could lead to a crisis for the organisation if such goods or services are found to be faulty or used incorrectly? What are the key risks associated with "faulty" supplied goods or services being passed on to customers?

• How can changes in the operational pattern of key customers and suppliers impact on the organisational operations?

• Are there any health, safety or environmental implications associated with the organisation's operations?

Operational threats are more probable than many of the other threat types and could manifest themselves in a great number of ways including complete loss of production and potential business failure, together with the possible life safety and environmental implications of some process failures.

The actions of people

Whether unintentional or not, the actions of people can lead to a variety of crises affecting both the organisation itself or outwardly caused threats to external persons or organisations. Many human resource agencies and experts will be able to provide information on this subject. The following considerations could help in identifying significant threats. Note that the list is not exhaustive.

- What is the possibility that one or more key personnel quit or are long term absent from the organisation at any one time? Are there any work related or social activities where groups of key personnel are involved. Activities may include lottery syndicates and adventure holidays?

- Are there any groups or individuals within the organisation who have shown unusual or aggressive behaviour towards the organisation or towards others within the organisation? Such behaviour could result in unwanted publicity or even increased safety risks as personnel can become preoccupied.

- Does the corporate culture allow or even encourage attitudes that could lead to actions being taken against the best interests of the organisation? Such actions, could include internet usage that may lead to publicity of confidential information or "malicious humour" being misinterpreted by external parties.

- Do individuals within the organisation hold detailed knowledge of the organisation and its operations, key projects, etc. that is relied upon yet has not been transposed for common use?

- How easily could a viral infection or other form of illness spread within the organisation? How could a pandemic outbreak impact on the organisation?

- Has the organisation made any decisions that could disadvantage any individuals, groups or organisations?

- Could the organisation be associated with national or sector based activities that could cause offence to individuals, groups, organisations or nations?

Actions arising from people can be typically hard to assess but can have some of the most devastating outcomes to many organisations. Key examples can include corporate defamation to mass illness to the poaching of key staff by competitors.

5 THREAT ANALYSIS

The earlier Chapters provide a number of considerations based on a range of possible threats to the organisation. From each of these categories of threat, there may be a number of ways in which each threat may manifest itself, i.e. the types of risk that an organisation could face. From this list, an assessment of the possible outcomes can be made.

Note that it may be found that one threat type may manifest in one or more ways, each of which may lead to a number of possible outcomes. Similarly, a number of threats and the derived risk manifestations could result in a shared possible outcome. This is illustrated in Figure 3.

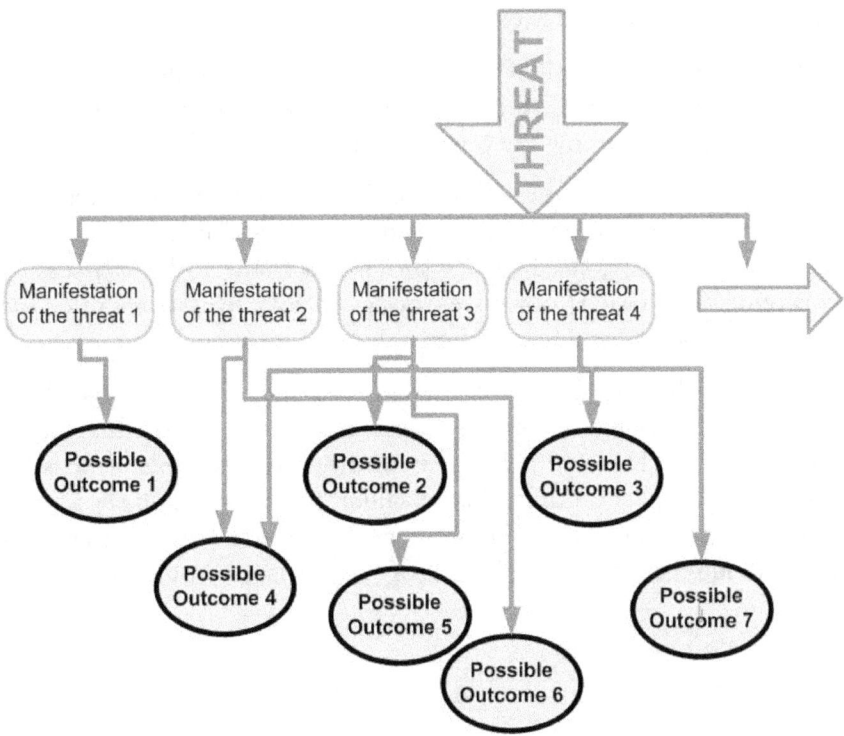

Figure 3: Identification of possible outcomes

As an example, the intentional threat of terrorism could lead to arson or explosion. The arson example could lead to fire damage to parts of the organisation. Similarly, this may be the same outcome as an operational process failure leading to equipment burn out.

Another example is where an economic downturn or recession could lead to clients delaying payment which could then lead to short term cash flow difficulties, worsening relations with clients and suppliers, and loss of key personnel attracted to "better performing companies"; an outcome shared by other threats.

This three tier assessment approach can help derive a list of possible outcomes, some of which may not have been thought about prior to the analysis. The list should be unique to an organisation although organisations working within the same sector and/or located in the same vicinity are likely to have similar lists. The size and range of the list is likely to be proportionate to the level of detail to which the organisation has assessed itself and the level of risk from threats the organisation is exposed to.

Once a complete list of threats and their corresponding possible outcomes is prepared, there will be a need to prioritize these outcomes based on how the organisation could be affected.

As an aid to this appraisal, each of the outcomes could be assessed against the organisational "risk based" objectives such as life safety, business continuity, etc. Figure 4 provides a framework for assessing corporate "risk based" objectives, designed for the assessment of the key requirements for a fire strategy.

This can be equally used to assess crisis management objectives. Each possible outcome can be assessed against each of the sixteen factors given. This can help focus on how, for example, a possible output may impact on the safety of building occupants, on short term business operations or on the protection of fixed assets. This analysis will provide the assessor with a list of "risk" assessed outcomes.

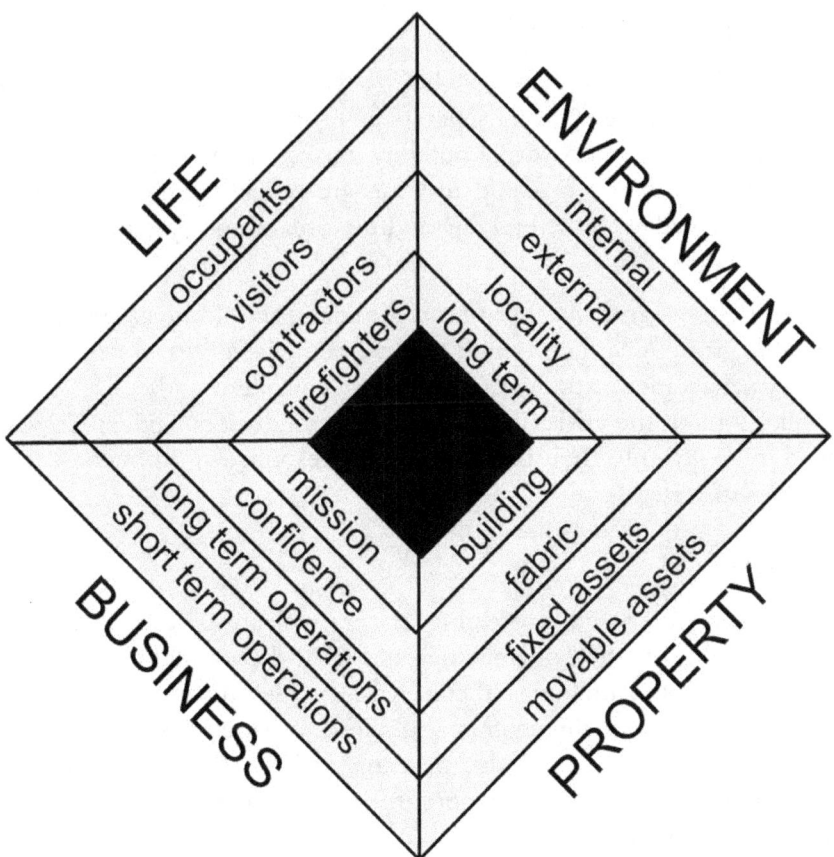

Figure 4: Risk based objectives matrix

Life

Life safety is broken down into four sub-objectives. Occupants of the building will have at least some knowledge of the organisation culture and rules as well as the building layout and emergency requirements. The plan will need to identify those threats that will directly and indirectly affect this group and the types of crisis that could result.

Visitors will not have the same level of knowledge as occupants but, as is the case with many public buildings including airports, railway stations and hospitals, may form the highest population group at any one time. The general public, and their protection against various forms of threat will normally be a fundamental requirement for any organisation that incorporates this group in sizeable numbers within their infrastructure.

Contractors, those persons who are working on the building and infrastructure, are listed as a separate category. The reason for this is that they may be in a part of a building during an emergency situation where it is just not possible to evacuate quickly. They may have partial knowledge of the building and the organisation's requirements and procedures.

Firefighters, and all other first responders, should be assessed as a separate group, bearing in mind that they may be a critical part of the crisis management strategy. As well as considering the life safety implications of the crisis on emergency responders, consideration will need to be given to their part in the crisis response and how best this can be supported.

Property

Property, or asset, protection covers objectives related to the organisation's building or buildings and what these buildings contain. Starting with the buildings themselves, an identification should be made of the type of threats that could lead to damage or destruction. This consideration should also be expanded to identify if access to those buildings could be temporarily or permanently affected by certain types of crisis.

The internal fabric if the building is treated as a separate issue. Sometimes the linings, which could be ancient frescos, may be more valuable than the building itself. This may be covered as part of the risk management process but some threats, and the corresponding crises that may result, may override these measures.

Similar considerations need to be made for fixed assets, whether this includes valuable manufacturing and processing plant or fixed computer systems. Movable assets are considered separately as they may require a different type of thinking. This will include works of art, special tools and plant, and mobile computer equipment.

Business

Business protection and continuity is always recognized as a critical objectives for most organisations yet, in more than a few cases, little is done to provide adequate levels of protection. Initial consideration should be given to how threats may impact on short term operations (hours and days following the crisis) and how they could also affect those operations in the longer term (weeks and months). Business also relies upon confidence; the confidence of its clients, its suppliers and any other stakeholders affected by the possible crisis. It is not just the crisis itself that could adversely impact on confidence but how it is handled. Moving to the "mission" sub-objective, some crises could cause more fundamental changes to the business and impact on the business strategy.

Environment

The environment, and how it could be adversely affected by a crisis, is an area that could be overlooked. It is possible that "environmental concern" triggered litigation will become more commonplace, where the environment could be unwittingly damaged or destroyed by actions of an organisation. Consideration should be given to how some forms of crisis could impact on the environment both within, and external to, the organisation's building(s). The impact could derive both from the crisis and from methods used to control the crisis. This may also apply to potential damage to the locality, which could include issues such as pollution of the local area. It is possible that there are longer term aspects which may impact on the ecology of the area, or the long term health of those affected by the crisis.

By undertaking the threat analysis and using the context of each of the elements of the objectives matrix, additional dimensions of how threats can impact on the organisation may be ascertained.

6 RISK MITIGATION

Measures should be taken to limit the possibility and impact of the associated "risk assessed" outcomes to the organisation. This can be achieved in one of two ways; Preventing an event or a combination of events from occurring, or protecting against those events and the possible outcomes.

To assist with the assessment, and to help determine where prevention and protection resources are best applied, each of the threat outcomes should be assessed in terms of probability and impact. A form of scoring system could be used, undertaken by the group preparing the crisis management plan.

Once each of the threats have been assessed, these could be plotted on a "probability/impact" matrix such as the one shown in Figure 5. It is those outputs that exist in the top right hand quadrant that will demand the most attention when determining prevention and protection measures, then the top left-hand quadrant, then the bottom right-hand quadrant and finally the bottom left-hand quadrant, where the perceived risk is lowest. Note that prevention techniques will typically move the risk outputs to the left, whilst protection techniques will lower them.

Prevention

For each of the risks identified, there should be efforts made to prevent their occurrence. The measures taken will be commensurate with the type and probability of the risk and with the perceived impact to the organisation. The key objective behind risk prevention is to go back to the root causes of the threats identified and remove or reduce these factors and the way they may manifest themselves, at the source. For each of the threat categories identified earlier, the following gives "risk prevention" examples:

Intentional: The instatement of physical or manned security measures; the placing of premises away from identified "hotspots"; the creation of "positive" messages about the organisation; the removal of any "extremism" within the organisation; involvement in community crime prevention schemes.

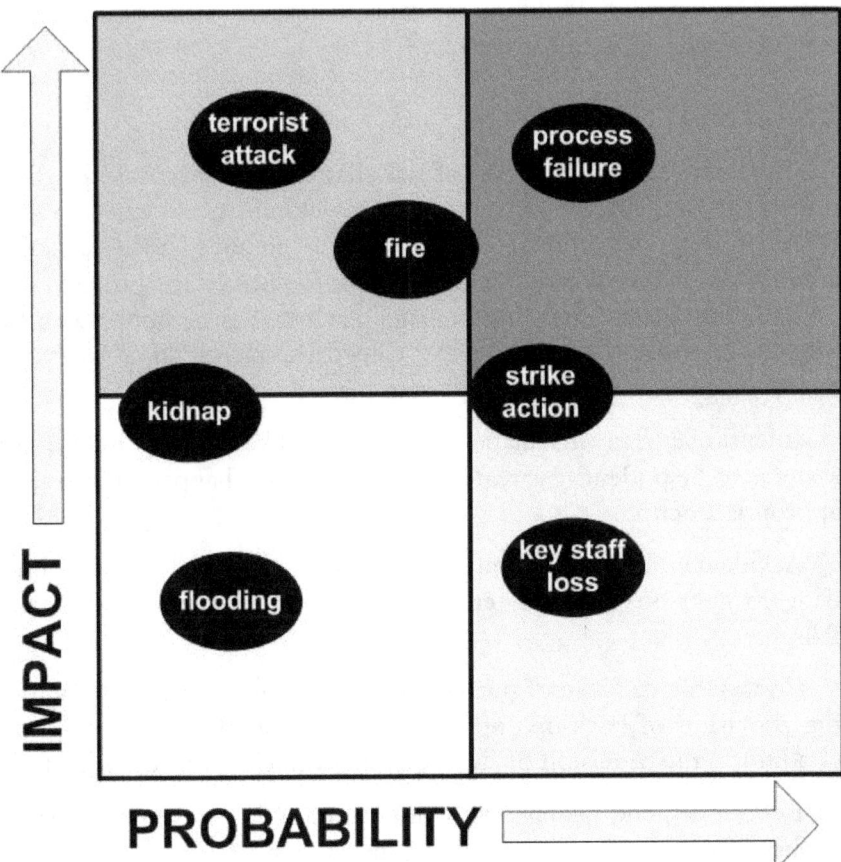

Figure 5: Probability / Impact Matrix

Accidental: Adherence to health and safety guidelines; the introduction of "zero tolerance" safety schemes; the rectification of any identified non-compliances following a risk assessment.

Environmental: The locating of offices, plant etc. in areas away from possible environmental threats; the spreading of operations over different geographical areas.

Economic: The use of financial, commercial and economic risk reduction techniques and systems.

Personal: The preparation and use of appropriate contracts of employment; the use of open and communicative management styles; the use of team working.

Operational: Proper maintenance of equipment and processes; proper equipment training regimes; continual risk assessments; remote regular IT data back-ups.

Protection

There will always be a level of risk that cannot be removed by the undertaking of risk prevention measures alone. As a next step and before setting up actions to cope with a possible crisis scenario, additional measures should be put into place to protect the organisation against unwanted events, such that their impact can be limited. For each of the threat categories identified above, the following gives "risk protection" examples:

Intentional: The installation of fire, CCTV, security and other systems to help identify threats as and when they happen and to take appropriate actions.

Accidental: The use of safety systems and arrangements to limit danger to persons and to cater for the outcome of possible accidents, falls, etc.

Environmental: Use of protective walls or bunds against flooding; the provision of back-up supplies in the event of extreme weather conditions; the provision of snow clearing vehicles and equipment.

Economic: The taking out of insurance policies against possible economic events; the use of hedging instruments.

Personal: The use of third party HR agencies; the taking out of HR related insurance plans.

Operational: Access to back-up process equipment; the arrangement of back-up power supplies; IT "hot standby" facilities.

7 PRE-CRISIS PREPARATION

The basis of any crisis management plan is to prepare for an impending crisis. The preparation will need to consider a number of facets that, combined together, will be the basis of the plan. These should then be tested to ensure that the plan is fit for purpose. Key to any crisis management plan are the following:

- A command and control structure.
- A communications network.
- A set of operating procedures and instructions.
- Supporting intelligence.
- Resource planning and utilisation.
- Testing and exercising regime.

Command and Control Structure

A formal structure should be set up to deal with a crisis. This structure will vary from organisation to organisation but there should be a clear pre-agreed route for decision making and the subsequent tactics and actions taken. For a small organisation, there may be a simple two tier system whereby, for example, company directors are consulted to what actions are taken and they give the corresponding orders to those who will undertake those activities deemed appropriate in the circumstances.

For larger organisations or for those involved in crisis response, a three tiered command structure may be relevant. An example of this is the gold, silver and bronze levels often used by those involved with emergency response. An example of how this can be set up is as follows:

Gold command is the level at which strategic decision making is used. Gold command personnel will have overall control of their organisation's resources and will allocate these resources as an event progresses.

Silver command is the level at which tactical decisions are made following the strategic direction given by gold command. These are then converted into a series of tasks that are completed by the bronze level personnel. Silver may be in control of some of the resources available. They may not become directly involved in dealing with the incident itself.

Bronze command undertakes the activities as instructed by silver command. They will utilise the designated resources to help control the incident or to undertake tasks designed to assist with any subsequent recovery.

Although the above command structure is designed around incident response by the emergency services it can also be used for other crisis situations that are not incident based. For example, where a financial or economic crisis is looming and could impact on the organisation, the gold command would be the board of directors, silver would be the principal managers such as the financial controller, and bronze would be those within the company or external to it (such as clerks, financial dealers, accountants, etc.) who will take such actions as directed to alleviate the situation. Similarly, where organisational personnel are involved in actions that could lead to problems for the organisation, bronze could be the HR department.

Communications

As a crisis can occur at any time, a robust and resilient communication structure should be established to ensure that those who need to be involved in the crisis management process are contactable when required. Furthermore, parties external to the command and control function may need to be kept informed of the situation to minimize duress and to avoid misinformation and miscommunication. The following paragraphs provide some points to consider.

The Command Team: A method or methods of communication for those involved in the gold, silver and bronze structure. It should be appreciated that some may be off site so alternative communication methods may be required. Consideration should be given to communication between those at the same command level and between command levels. Furthermore, there may be need for access to intelligence to aid with any decision making, which will need to be planned for. Organisations should also consider whether they require secure communications at command levels, to allow sensitive matters to be discussed and acted on without fear of compromise.

Other organisational personnel: All those affected by a crisis and especially those working for the organisation will need to be informed of what is happening and what is being done to resolve the situation. This could be communicated by a telephone tree arrangement, by fax or email or via the company website.

External emergency responders: In the event of an incident based crisis, and where the crisis management strategy relies on external intervention there should be a clear procedure in place.

Friends and family: Where a crisis may involve danger to persons, there may be a need to contact those friend or family members who are affected. This should be made in a timely manner to avoid information arriving from other sources that could be corrupted or incorrect. Consequently, contact details will need to be readily available to those involved in the Command Structure.

Clients and suppliers: In order to preserve relationships subsequent to the handling of the crisis, it may be advisable that key stakeholders in the organisation such as clients and suppliers are kept advised of the situation. As well as limiting any potential longer term damage to the organisation's operations it can create additional confidence in the abilities of the organisation in a time of crisis.

The wider community: Where deemed appropriate, those who could be impacted by the crisis may need to be kept informed as events unfold. This could be those living or working in the vicinity of the organisation or those who operate in a related industry.

Communications with press and media: Where a crisis is likely to be of interest to a wider audience, a pre-planned response should be established. Failure to adequately inform the press and media with the right message could lead to misinformation being circulated to all those groups listed above, together with other possible affected groups. Pre-arranged messages from agreed sources are one method but, in many cases, this aspect will need close management. For those organisations without such dedicated resources, public relations agencies may be an answer.

Operating procedures and instructions

Pre-drafted operating procedures and instructions can help minimize confusion, improve consistency of approach, and help in the speed of response to a crisis. The type, number and format of these procedures will vary from organisation to organisation but there a number of considerations to be made:

• Are the procedures/instructions relevant to the organisation? Generic Standard Operating Procedures may be easy to obtain but may need to be modified before they can be properly used.

• Are the procedures/instructions relevant to the risks? It should be ensured that the risks identified by the threat assessment as most likely to occur are covered.

• Are the procedures / instructions in a format that they can be promptly and properly used? Can they be easily deciphered in a crisis situation by those needing to use them? Any procedures or instructions will need to be to the point and not too wordy. A flow chart approach is often a good way to present the key steps in a process.

• Are the procedures / instructions accessible to those who will need them in a crisis? Paper based procedures / instructions may be the easiest way of collecting procedures but may be stored in a place where they cannot be quickly accessed when required.

Supporting intelligence

Together with the operational procedures and instructions identified above, there may be a need to refer to more generic information to assist with any decision making. Such information may take a variety of forms including company standards, manuals of good practice, drawings and layouts, address lists etc. These should be in a form to allow for rapid access to relevant data. Furthermore they should be in a form and format to allow accessibility by various persons involved in crisis management and control.

Resources

For every crisis, there will be a need for a set of resources to assist with crisis management and control. Resources may be tangible, such as the use of equipment or may be less obvious when they may be in the form of specialist advice. The following forms of resource may be appropriate:

Human resource: This will include personnel involved in the command structure, other support personnel required to assist in response and/or recovery. This could also include external organisations such as engineers, consultants, accountants, lawyers and PR companies.

Equipment: This could include IT and communication equipment and systems, some of which may need to be resilient; personal protective equipment; machinery; tools, etc. There may also be a need for special early response items to aid with initial crisis scenarios, such as grab boxes.

Plant: This could include access equipment such as towers, cranes or ladders, and extrication equipment and systems.

The Plan will need to identify the resources required for any given crisis, their accessibility and availability in the event of a crisis. It is understood that ownership of certain resources may not be commercially or logistically feasible. In such cases, a pre-agreed method of procuring such resources at short notice should be established.

8   RESPONDING TO A CRISIS

The way we respond to a crisis, especially in the early stages, will determine how successful we have been in minimizing its impact. The objective is to control the duration of a crisis and to contain the level of resource applied. In ideal circumstances, when a crisis arises, actions are put effortlessly into place, following the plan closely without encountering unexpected or exceptional issues. In reality, everything may not go according to plan. Figure 6 gives three different examples of a crisis response profile, with three very different outcomes.

Profile A is an example of a crisis management plan that proves to be totally effective. The curve itself is similar to a "bell curve" shape. As a crisis is identified, resources are quickly put into place and applied until the crisis is contained. They continue to be applied until the crisis is resolved and then can be relatively quickly removed.

Profile B is possibly more realistic and is shaped as a distorted and elongated bell curve. In this case, the crisis plan commences as with profile A. However, as progress is made, additional events may occur which divert attention from the initial crisis, these "unexpected" additions to the scenario can utilise resources originally designated to deal with the initial crisis, or additional resources are drawn in at short notice, with minimal if any pre-planning. The result is likely to lead to a delay in resolving the crisis with additional resources applied than originally deemed necessary.

Profile C could be the result of a poorly planned crisis response or where there is no form of crisis planning. In this case, there is a slow buildup of resources usage, probably due to the crisis scenario not being recognised for some time, or early decisions not being made as to what to do next. As the crisis becomes apparent, and possibly due to a "knee-jerk" reaction, resources are applied hastily without aligning these to any form of plan. In such scenarios, there is a good chance that secondary and tertiary crises result with the need to cater for these by ever more resource allocation.

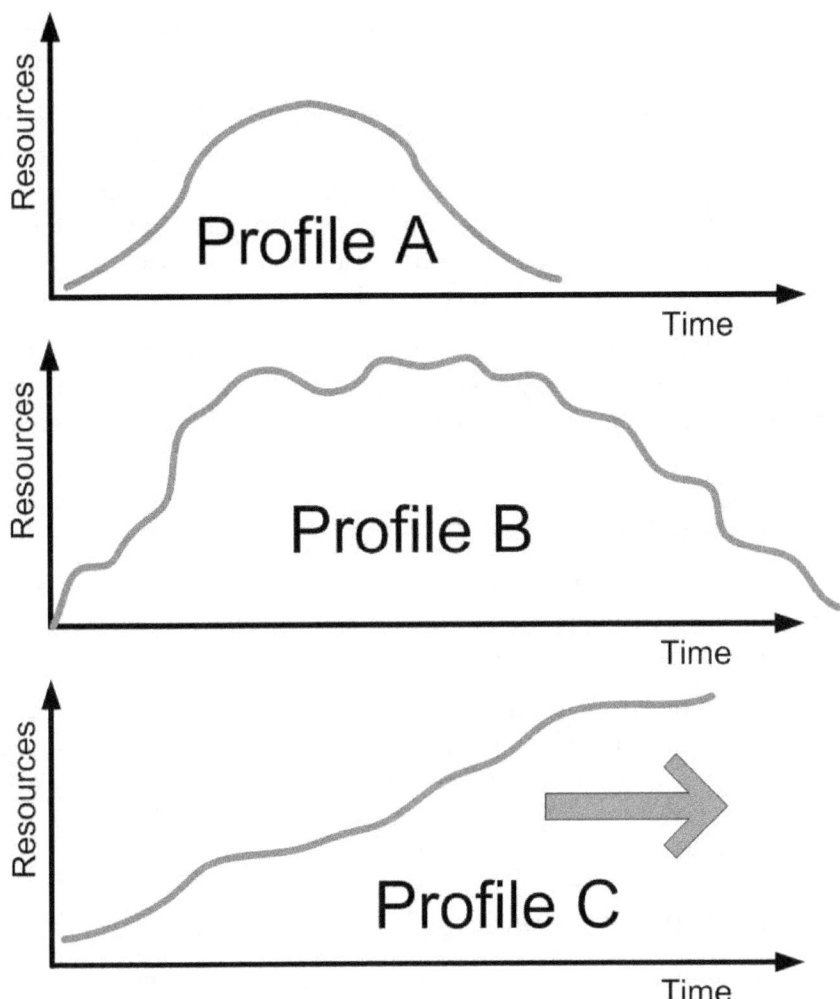

Figure 6: Crisis response profiles

The consequence is that the crisis is never really resolved although resource allocation may be reduced over time as the main and most obvious components of the crisis would have appeared to have settled.

If we look at the resource / time allocation under the curves, we will note that this would be a good approximation to what the cost of crisis response would be. For Profile C, the implication is that the final cost will never be easily resolved. Furthermore, the longer a crisis continues the greater the cost could be in terms of impact on business operations, asset loss, environmental damage and most importantly, life.

Concluding from the above, the priority is to limit the duration of a crisis. This can only be achieved by the utilisation of a pre-planned response based on thorough pre-crisis preparation and followed by an effective crisis recovery programme (see Chapter 9). In addition, the crisis management response should allow for the management of unforeseen issues as described later in this Chapter.

The manner and method of response will be determined by the requirements of the organisation but the key features should be Included in the crisis management plan. The following provides some of the issues to be considered.

Is it a crisis?

As an incident, event or other issue is experienced, a decision should be made quickly as to whether it demands a formal crisis management response or can be handled in a less formalized way.

The decision can be made at any level, commensurate with the event. Where there is doubt or confusion, this decision should be passed up the chain of command until a firm decision can be made. The process for this together with any crisis defining criteria should be incorporated into the response plan.

Establishing and enabling the response team

Once it has been confirmed that the situation requires a crisis response, a process for contacting and rallying key personnel will need to be established. Initially, those in the Command and Control chain should be contacted and moved to their respective agreed positions. For some incident or event based crisis situations, an emergency crisis response room or rooms may need to be established. These are places where decision making and coordination of response are managed. Where organisations believe that such resources are relevant, further information can be obtained from emergency response authorities or from a number of professional sources.

Initiating and maintaining the response

For a properly controlled crisis response, the skill will be in providing the right type and level of resource to specific parts of the crisis, as and when required. For this reason, all decisions will need to be made at the strategic level, from the outset of the response to its agreed completion. Issues relevant to ongoing decision making may include:

- the crisis status at any point in its duration.
- the resources still available.
- any unforeseen issues or conditions.
- the communications status.
- ensuring external parties such as "press and media" and "friends and families" are updated as per the agreed plan.
- an assessment of probable outcomes based on current knowledge.

Assessing the Status

At the commencement of the crisis response and continually or regularly throughout the crisis duration, the status of the crisis will need to be evaluated so that appropriate actions and resource allocations can be directed to optimise their effect. The assessment may include some, or all, of the following:

- The key features of the crisis together with possible outcomes.
- The geographical area affected.
- Casualties – number and type.
- The type and severity of damage to infrastructure and assets.
- A safety risk assessment of the situation for those involved and for emergency responders.
- Resources utilised – type and quantity.
- The physical and psychological impact of actions and decisions made on all those involved in the crisis response.
- An assessment of the operational and environmental impact of

intervention tasks.

- The longer term implications for decisions made.

Note that both incident and non-incident based crises may require additional status assessment by relevant industry professionals such as PR companies, legal professionals, etc.

Communications monitoring

There should be a method of recording and storing of communications between the command and control structure, and with external parties, whether it be in verbal or written format. There should also be the ability for those at the strategic level to monitor such communications, preferably in real time. As well as assisting with the crisis response, the communications can be used after the crisis for any debrief or as an audit trail.

Handling the unexpected or unwanted

As highlighted earlier, a planned crisis response may be hampered by unexpected situations. Such conditions may result from the best (and worst) intentions of people or from risks or hazards not properly appreciated at the onset of the crisis response. Although the crisis response plan cannot be expected to cope with every eventuality, the provision of appropriate back-up information or intelligence can help with decision making. The following paragraphs provide a few examples of such situations.

- Voyeurs, do-gooders and other groups unintentionally, or intentionally, hamper the crisis response efforts. This may be in the form of turning up on site, or offering their support via "swamped" communications channels.

- VIPs or dignitaries lend their support to the crisis response by turning up without warning to "assist". This can divert attention, especially at the strategic command level but must be properly handled especially as press and media are likely to be in accompaniment. This is particularly the case for senior executive personnel, who may not have a formal role in the management of a crisis but who feel obliged to intervene. Crisis roles for these personnel should be explicitly defined in advance.

• New hazards, not previously envisaged or allowed for, are identified and are not covered by any plan or procedure. Background information on the hazard type, or how the hazard may have been handled in prior crises, could be invaluable.

• Key parts of the command and control chain are not available, possibly due to illness or vacation. To cover for such circumstances, the plan should either allow for alternative personnel or for remote real time communications.

Documenting the response

A complete audit trail should be maintained to identify the decisions made at every step of the crisis together with any reasoning of information behind the decision. Such supporting information should include the communications log.

9 RECOVERING FROM A CRISIS

Once it is deemed that a crisis is over, there will be a number of actions and considerations that will need to be taken to allow recovery from a crisis so that the organisation can revert back, as far as possible, to its pre-crisis condition. However, there may be some aspects of the crisis that may take longer to overcome and some that may lead to a permanent change of circumstances. Nevertheless, a formalised process of recovery should be followed through in all cases. A recovery process may allow for the following:

• Those involved in the response phase command structure should formally sign off with positive confirmation that this has happened at all tiers and by all groups. Where there is deemed a necessity to have the same command and control function for the recovery phase, or this is to be handed to a secondary team, then this should be incorporated within the plan.

• Any residual physical risks should be contained or removed to avoid further danger to persons, buildings or equipment.

• Those persons involved in the crisis should be provided with ongoing assistance, whether it be medical, psychological advisorial or legal. Such care should be given, where practicable, away from the scene of the crisis. Fatalities should be properly treated with cognizance made of any special circumstances related to faith, nationality, etc.

• All those affected by the crisis should be formally debriefed. This debrief should advise of the current status, what will happen as a consequence, and any relevant safety or follow up issues.

• Ongoing communications to all stakeholders of the crisis should be maintained until it is determined to no longer be necessary. This may be made in various forms but the messages given should be consistent.

• A chronological diary of events and of decisions made should be formulated using the information obtained from the crisis response (see Chapter 8). In conjunction with this, interviews with those involved in the crisis should be made at an early enough opportunity to avoid key factors from being forgotten or misinterpreted.

- All resources used should be assessed and formally retired. Equipment, plant and vehicles should be returned to their original positions. Any equipment that did not perform as intended should be formally identified and follow up actions should be decided upon.

- Any business continuity and salvage procedures should be implemented.

- Where deemed appropriate, the showing of appreciation to those who have assisted with the crisis can be helpful and improve morale.

10 TESTING AND EXERCISING THE PLAN

As crises are relatively rare events, the likelihood is that the crisis management plan cannot be properly validated unless it has been tested. Testing will provide confirmation or not that the plan is working and will help highlight factors that were not thought about in the preparation stages. Testing can be coordinated and undertaken by the organisation itself but it is normally recommended for a more robust arrangement, external parties experienced in the subject matter are utilised.

Operating procedure testing

This is the simplest form of testing and will involve a step by step analysis of operating procedures and the corresponding support structure to ensure that key elements have not been missed out and that the expected results are likely to be delivered.

Scenario playing

This is where one or more scenarios (possibly derived via the threat analysis) are played out with one or more persons involved in the command and control process. Scenarios are raised by those outside of the command structure and the idea is to use information available, possibly in the form of operating procedures, to follow through the process and highlight deficiencies or errors as the test unfolds. Resource allocation is likely to be simulated.

Table-top exercises

This form of exercise will normally require the participation of the full command and control structure and could include other parties who may be called upon to assist in a crisis. One or more scenarios are normally chosen and researched in advance by crisis facilitators who will then, at a chosen time, relay the crisis scenario to the crisis response teams and will continue to update them with new information. They will then monitor the activity on behalf of the organisation but will not participate. Resources may be simulated although communication channels and arrangements should be as to be used in a real crisis. A Table-top exercise can be a robust test of most types of crisis situation and can deliver very meaningful lessons.

Full-scale exercises

A full-scale exercise is a complete simulation of an actual crisis in real time. It will involve the same principles as the table-top exercise but will also introduce, as far as possible, the practical aspects of the crisis tested. Furthermore, live resources will be used. A full scale exercise will be the most effective manner to test a crisis scenario and is particularly useful and relevant for incident and event based crises.

11 REVIEW AND MAINTENANCE OF THE PLAN

The plan should be reviewed on a periodic basis, and following any changes that are likely to have an impact on it. This will include changes to the organisation, its structure and infrastructure and macroeconomic, operational, environmental, cultural and political events. Furthermore, reviews should be made following the results of tests and exercises and in the event the plan is used in a real crisis scenario.

It is recommended that those with responsibility for the plan undertake an in house review annually. It is also recommended that a more formal review is undertaken within every five years by persons knowledgeable in crisis management planning.

The plan should be viewed as a live document and thus should be controlled as such in accordance with a recognised quality system.

ABOUT THE AUTHOR

PAUL BRYANT is a British fire strategist, a chartered fire and electrical engineer and a business entrepreneur. He has built up an international reputation for his approach to the subject of fire engineering and for the fire codes and guidance documents he has written. Paul started his career with a London based fire insurance organisation known as "The Fire Offices' Committee".

He then moved to the UK's Loss Prevention Council before taking on the key role of Head of Fire Engineering at London Underground – the oldest underground railway in the world. Paul went on to form Kingfell in the mid-1990s and grew it from a single manned operation to a multi-million pound "fire" one stop shop – combining consultancy and systems engineering. He also explored combining fire engineering with crisis management.

Paul divested his interests in systems engineering in 2011 and now concentrates on developing a specialist international fire and risk consultancy for complex buildings and infrastructures. He continues to lecture on his chosen field around the world.

Kingfell offers a range of specialist fire and risk services. Check them out at www.kingfell.com.

www.ingramcontent.com/pod-product-compliance
Lightning Source LLC
Chambersburg PA
CBHW071541170526
45166CB00004B/1504